The Teacher's Secret
and Other Folk Tales

LEVEL ONE   400 HEADWORDS

OXFORD
UNIVERSITY PRESS

Great Clarendon Street, Oxford OX2 6DP

Oxford University Press is a department of the University of Oxford.
It furthers the University's objective of excellence in research, scholarship,
and education by publishing worldwide in

Oxford New York

Auckland Cape Town Dar es Salaam Hong Kong Karachi
Kuala Lumpur Madrid Melbourne Mexico City Nairobi
New Delhi Shanghai Taipei Toronto

With offices in

Argentina Austria Brazil Chile Czech Republic France Greece
Guatemala Hungary Italy Japan Poland Portugal Singapore
South Korea Switzerland Thailand Turkey Ukraine Vietnam

OXFORD and OXFORD ENGLISH are registered trade marks of
Oxford University Press in the UK and in certain other countries

ISBN: 978 0 19 424768 9 BOOK
ISBN: 978 0 19 424732 0 BOOK AND MULTIROM PACK
MULTIROM NOT AVAILABLE SEPARATELY

Printed in China

ACKNOWLEDGEMENTS

Illustrations and cover by: Martina Farrow

The publisher would like to thank the following for permission to reproduce photographs: Getty
Images p38 (Wedding/Stone/Bob Thomas), p39 (Turkish wedding) by kind permission of
Candan and Ömer Sancak, p39 (Korean wedding) by kind permission of Min-Young Kim
and Dae-Ho Kim.

The Activities and Projects in this book were written by Janet Hardy-Gould

DOMINOES

Series Editors: Bill Bowler and Sue Parminter

The Teacher's Secret and Other Folk Tales

Retold by Joyce Hannam

Illustrated by Martina Farrow

Joyce Hannam has taught English in several European countries including Greece, Spain, Turkey and the Czech Republic. She now lives in York, in the north of England, and works mainly with Japanese and Chinese university students, and business people from Europe. She has written a number of other stories for students of English, including *The Death of Karen Silkwood* in the Oxford Bookworms Library, and *The Curse of the Mummy* in the Dominoes series.

OXFORD
UNIVERSITY PRESS

Contents

BEFORE READING

1 The six tales in this book come from different countries. What are they about? Match these sentences about the stories with the pictures.

a ☐ Fanta-Ghirò lives in Italy. She wants to join the army and help her father.

b ☐ Nasreddin is a poor man in Turkey. He lives next to a rich man called Ahmet.

c ☐ A Korean teacher has a secret. His students want to know about it.

d ☐ Princess Tara lives in India. She doesn't want to marry.

e ☐ One summer Prince Frederick visits Poland and meets a beautiful young woman called Irka.

f ☐ Fatima lives in Syria. One day she reads a sign in Ali's shop.

Women are clever, but men think faster.

2 What do you think? Tick the boxes.

Which people are cleverer . . . ?

a

☐ women
☐ men

b
☐ rich people
☐ poor people

c
☐ students

☐ teachers

Fanta-Ghirò

King Marco lived in Italy. He had three daughters – and no sons!

'What's the matter?' asked Fanta-Ghirò, his youngest daughter, one day.

'It's this letter from King Luca of Randazzo,' said her father. 'He wants to **fight** me and be king here too. He's sending his **army**. What can I do? I'm old with no sons to fight for me.'

'I can fight for you!' his oldest daughter said.

'But armies don't like women **generals**,' said King Marco.

'I can wear men's clothes,' she said, and later that day she left with the army.

After some time, she saw some tall trees. 'Look!' she cried. 'I can **cook** dinner for all the army with **wood** from only one of those trees.'

'Cook?!' cried the man next to her, 'The general is a woman!' Everyone laughed. The oldest daughter went home at once, and the army came home behind her.

---

king the most important man in a country

fight (*past* **fought**) to hit someone again and again

army a large number of people who fight for their country

general a very important person in an army

cook to make things for people to eat

wood the hard part of a tree

The next day the second sister left with the army. She said nothing when she saw the tall trees. Then they came to a river.

'Look!' she cried. 'I can **wash** the dirtiest shirts in that river and they're going to come out white again.'

'Wash?!' cried the man next to her, 'This general is a woman, too!'

When his second daughter came back, King Marco said, 'Oh no! I'm going to lose my country to King Luca!' 'Don't forget me!' said Fanta-Ghirò.

Fanta-Ghirò didn't talk on the road. 'This general is quiet,' thought the man next to her. 'But he **rides** and carries his **sword** well.'

wash to stop something being dirty   **sword** a long, sharp knife for fighting

ride (*past* **rode**) to go on a horse

Soon beautiful Fanta-Ghirò met King Luca and his army. 'Who are you?' he asked her. 'I'm King Marco's general,' she said. 'Shall we talk before we fight?' 'All right,' said Luca. 'But let's go to my **palace**.' Fanta-Ghirò asked the man next to her, Tonino, to go with her.

At his palace, Luca spoke to his mother. 'Perhaps King Marco's general is a woman, but how can I be **sure**?' His mother said, 'Take him to the sword room. Women aren't interested in swords.'

Then Luca's mother said, 'Take him into the garden and watch when he **picks** a flower. A woman puts a flower down the front of her dress. A man puts it behind his ear.'

But Fanta-Ghirò looked at the swords for hours.

But Fanta-Ghirò picked a yellow flower and put it behind her ear.

palace a big house where a king lives   **pick** to take something in your hand

sure when you feel that something is true

'What now?' asked Luca. 'She's a woman, I'm sure. Look at her beautiful face.'
'He loves the general,' his mother thought.
'Ask him to have dinner with you,' she told Luca. 'A man breaks his bread with his hands. A woman **cuts** her bread with a knife.'

But Fanta-Ghirò broke her bread with her hands.

After dinner the **queen** said, 'It's a hot night. Ask him to **swim** with you. Two men can swim together happily, but a woman is going to say 'no'.'

When Luca asked, Fanta-Ghirò said, 'Of course, I'd love to swim with you. But I'm tired and it's late. Let's do it tomorrow morning.'
And she went to her room.

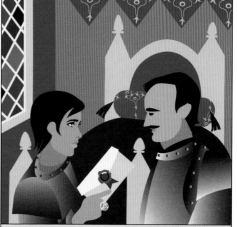

There Fanta-Ghirò wrote a letter. She called Tonino and said, 'Take this letter and go to stay with our army tonight. Early tomorrow morning, come back and give me the letter.'

cut (*past* **cut**) to make one big thing into a many little things with a knife

swim (*past* **swam**) to go through the water moving your arms and legs

queen the most important woman in a country

4

The next morning Fanta-Ghirò met Luca. 'Let's swim now,' he said. 'Wait!' she said, 'I can hear a horse and it's coming fast. Perhaps it's something important.'

Just then Tonino arrived and gave her the letter. Fanta-Ghirò read it.

'Oh, no!' she cried. 'My father's dying. I must leave. Let's talk tomorrow.' And she rode away at once.

Now Luca's mother was sure. 'Fanta-Ghirò *is* a woman. Go after her and see what she does,' she said to Luca.

Fanta-Ghirò went home. She put on women's clothes and spoke with her father in the palace garden. Luca went after her and listened from behind a tree.

'Father, I must go back to King Luca's palace tomorrow,' said Fanta-Ghirò. 'But he's very friendly now, and he isn't going to fight us.'

Then Luca came from behind the tree. 'You *are* a woman!' he cried happily. 'I knew it! Please be my wife and queen!'
'All right!' said Fanta-Ghirò. 'And our two countries can be one without a fight.'
King Marco laughed. 'Sometimes daughters are better than sons,' he said.

READING CHECK

Choose the correct words to complete the sentences.

a King Marco has three sons (daughters).

b King Luca wants to fight visit King Marco.

c The oldest daughter wants to sing cook for the army.

d The second daughter wants to make wash clothes for the army.

e At first Fanta-Ghirò asks to fight talk to King Luca.

f ' Women Men aren't interested in swords,' says King Luca's mother.

g Fanta-Ghirò breaks cuts the bread.

h Tonino brings a letter sword to Fanta-Ghirò.

i In the end King Luca wants Fanta-Ghirò to be his general wife .

WORD WORK

1 These words don't match the pictures. Correct them.

· ~~king~~ ·

a ..palace..

· queen ·

b ....

· wood ·

c ....

· army ·

d ....

· palace ·

e ....

· general ·

f ....

2 Use the words from the sword to complete the sentences.

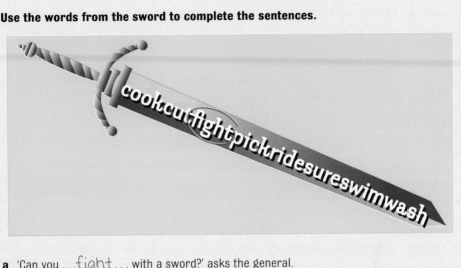

cookcutfightpickrideswimwash

a 'Can you ...*fight*... with a sword?' asks the general.

b 'It's very hot today. Let's go to the river and . . . .'

c 'I can't . . . . well. So I usually eat sandwiches.'

d 'Mum, can you . . . . this shirt? It's dirty.'

e 'Those flowers are beautiful. Can I . . . . one for my hair?'

f 'I . . . . my bicycle to school every day.'

g 'You can't . . . . wood with a sword!'

h 'Fanta-Ghirò is a woman. I'm . . . . !' thinks King Luca.

GUESS WHAT

The next story happens in Turkey. Here are two of the people in it. Tick the boxes.

Who . . .	Nasreddin	Ahmet
a . . . is poor?	☐	☐
b . . . is rich?	☐	☐
c . . . prays to God?	☐	☐
d . . . wants to get more money?	☐	☐
e . . . finds a bag of gold?	☐	☐
f . . . is a good neighbour?	☐	☐

One Thousand Gold Coins

pray to speak privately to God

God an important being who never dies and who decides what happens in the world

poor without money; something you say when you feel sorry for someone

gold an expensive yellow metal

coin metal money

exactly not a bigger or smaller number

neighbour a person who lives near you

wall something strong and thick that stands between two gardens or around something

throw (*past* **threw**) to make something move quickly through the air with your hands

ASREDDIN lived in Turkey. He was a good man, but not very rich, and his wife wasn't happy about it.

'You **pray** to **God** every day, but nothing changes. We are always **poor**!' she said. 'I don't understand it. God doesn't help us. Perhaps he doesn't like us!'

'Of course God likes us,' answered Nasreddin. 'He loves everyone. Be quiet, wife!'

But his wife never stopped talking about money. In the end, Nasreddin prayed to God: 'Please send me a thousand **gold coins**. Then my wife can be happy. But remember, I don't want nine hundred and ninety-nine, and I don't want one thousand and one. I want **exactly** one thousand coins.'

Every morning Nasreddin prayed to God for his gold coins. His **neighbour** Ahmet, a rich man, heard him over the garden **wall** every day. He laughed and said to his wife: 'Listen! Nasreddin says he doesn't want nine hundred and ninety-nine gold coins. I can't understand him. Everybody wants gold and Nasreddin is very poor. I'm going to **throw** nine hundred and ninety-nine gold coins over the wall into his garden. What's he going to do then? Let's see.'

The next morning, when Nasreddin began praying, a bag of gold coins suddenly came over the garden wall and hit Nasreddin on the head.

Nasreddin opened the bag and then smiled.

'Come here, wife,' he called. 'Look! God *is* listening to me.' His wife laughed and sang.

An hour later, Ahmet came to the door.

'How are you, Nasreddin?' he asked. 'I can hear laughing and singing in your house.'

'We are happy,' answered Nasreddin, 'because God is good to us. Look,' he said and he opened the bag in his hand. 'I asked God for gold and here it is.'

Ahmet smiled.

'How many gold coins are in the bag exactly?' he asked. 'You asked for one thousand, I think. Let's **count** them.'

'Why?' asked Nasreddin. 'God can count, you know!'

But Ahmet didn't listen. He began to count carefully. Then he said, 'You can't have this gold, Nasreddin. There are nine hundred and ninety-nine coins here, not a thousand.'

'Is that right?' said Nasreddin. 'Then God knows about it, and one more coin is going to come later today. I'm sure of it.'

'Listen, Nasreddin,' Ahmet said. 'It's my gold. I threw it over the wall and you must give it back.'

'I can't do that,' answered Nasreddin. 'You don't understand. God is working through you.'

count to say the numbers of things

9

Now Ahmet was angry. 'I'm going to take you to **court**. I want my gold back!'

'All right,' said Nasreddin. 'Let's speak to the **judge** about it. But I can't go to court in these poor, dirty clothes. Can I wear your coat?'

Ahmet wanted to go to court at once because he wanted to get his gold back that day. So he gave his coat to Nasreddin.

'Now, let's go,' Ahmet said, and he walked out of the door.

'Wait a minute,' said Nasreddin. 'I'm an old man and the court is far from here. How can I walk there?'

Ahmet stopped. 'It's not far,' he said angrily.

'It is for me,' answered Nasreddin. 'I have a bad leg.'

'All right,' said Ahmet. 'You can have my horse for the day. Wait a minute.'

So Ahmet brought his horse for Nasreddin to ride.

'Now we can go to court,' said Ahmet. 'You can ride the horse. I'm going to walk!'

court the place where the people say when something is right or wrong

judge the person in a court who says when something is right or wrong

'Wife, watch my gold coins carefully,' said Nasreddin before he left. 'Because sooner or later God is going to send me one more coin.'

Nasreddin and Ahmet arrived at the court.

When the judge saw them he asked, 'Why are you here?'

'Because,' answered Ahmet, 'this man, Nasreddin, has nine hundred and ninety-nine of my gold coins! He must give them back to me.'

'Is this true?' the judge asked Nasreddin.

'No, it isn't,' answered Nasreddin. 'This money came to me from God because I prayed for it.'

He went nearer to the judge and said quietly to him, 'I'm sorry but this poor man, my neighbour, is **mad**. All of my things are his things, he thinks. Ask him about this coat.'

'Is this your coat?' the judge asked Ahmet.

'Of course it is,' answered Ahmet. 'I gave it to Nasreddin.'

'You see!' said Nasreddin quietly to the judge. 'Now, ask him about the horse.'

'Is this your horse, too?' asked the judge.

'Yes, it is,' answered Ahmet.

'Poor man,' said the judge. 'You don't need a court. You need a doctor. You must say sorry to Nasreddin, and give him one gold coin – at once!'

Nasreddin took the gold coin from Ahmet.

'I thank God for this,' he said happily. 'Now I have the last of my thousand coins.'

Nasreddin and Ahmet left the court and went home. Later, Nasreddin gave back the coat, the horse, and the thousand gold coins to Ahmet.

'These are your things,' said Nasreddin, and he smiled. 'But remember, never come between God and man again.'

mad thinking things that are not true

READING CHECK

Correct these sentences.

a Nasreddin's wife talks a lot about ~~food.~~ *money*

b Nasreddin prays to God for one hundred gold coins.

c Nasreddin's neighbour, Ahmet, is a very poor man.

d Ahmet throws a bag of coins into Nasreddin's house.

e There are a thousand gold coins in the bag.

f Ahmet gives his hat to Nasreddin.

g 'Nasreddin is mad,' thinks the judge.

h Ahmet must give two more gold coins to Nasreddin.

WORD WORK

1 Find nine more words from *One Thousand Gold Coins* in the wordsquare.

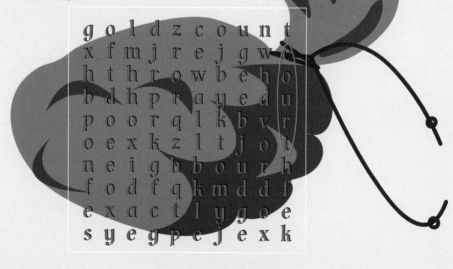

```
g o l d z c o u n t
x f m j r e j g w e
h t h r o w b e h o
b d h p r a y e d u
p o o r q l k b v r
o e x k z l t j o t
n e i g h b o u r h
f o d f q k m d d f
e x a c t l y g o e
s y e g p e j e x k
```

2 Use the words from Activity 1 to complete the sentences.

a He went to ... court ... because he took $10,000 from his father.

b The children are learning to . . . . from 1 to 10.

c 'Quickly! . . . . the ball to Fred; he's ready for it!'

d That woman lives in our street. She's our . . . .

e Give me . . . . two dollars; not two dollars and fifty cents.

f That film star always wears a very expensive . . . . watch.

g 'You must go to prison for five years,' said the . . . .

h They can't buy a lot of food because they are very . . . .

i After the accident they . . . . to God for help.

j You can't see the famous footballer's house. There's a big . . . . in front of it.

GUESS WHAT

The next story is about a school in Korea. This is the teacher and his students. Tick the boxes.

a The teacher is ...
 1 ☐ always friendly.
 2 ☐ very quiet.
 3 ☐ often angry.

b The students are ... the teacher.
 1 ☐ happy with
 2 ☐ afraid of
 3 ☐ interested in

c At the school the students learn to ...
 1 ☐ read and write.
 2 ☐ sing and dance.
 3 ☐ paint and cook.

The Teacher's Secret

Once there was an expensive **school** in Korea. The students there learned to read and write Chinese. They were all afraid of their teacher. He was an old man, and he was always angry when the students didn't do their school work well.

Sometimes when he watched his students at work, the teacher felt hungry. Then, he picked up a **basket** and ate something from it.

One day, one of his students, a little boy, asked, 'What are you eating, Teacher?' 'Oh!' he said quickly. 'It's my **secret**. It's good for old men, but it's **poison** for children!'

school students learn here

basket a box for carrying food

secret something that you don't tell to everybody

poison something that kills people when they eat or drink it

One morning, the teacher needed to go to the nearest town. Before he left he told his students, 'You must read and write without me all morning.'

After an hour, the students were tired of reading and writing.
'Let's look in the teacher's basket,' said the little boy. 'I want to know his secret.'
'Me too,' said his friend.

When they opened the basket, they found lots of nice **dried fruit** in it. 'That isn't poison!' said an older girl. 'I'm hungry,' said the little boy. And he took some fruit from the basket and began to eat it.

Then everybody took some of the teacher's fruit and ate it. Soon there was nothing in the basket.

dried fruit something like an apple or orange with no water in it that doesn't go bad quickly

'Oh dear! What are we going to do now?' the students asked. 'Our teacher is going to be very angry with us . . .'

The room was suddenly quiet. Then the little boy spoke. 'I have an **idea**!' he said. 'Can you help me?'

The students listened to him. Then they all **pushed over** the teacher's table. Black **ink** went all over the **floor** and the teacher's beautiful **ink stone** broke in half. 'Now **lie down** everybody,' said the little boy. All the students lay down on the floor.

That afternoon, the teacher came back from town. He walked into the room and shouted at once: 'What's the matter? Why are you all lying on the floor?'

idea something that you think

push over to move something strongly down onto the floor with your hands

ink you write with this

floor the place in a room where you stand and walk

ink stone you put water on this to make ink

lie down (*past* **lay**) to have all your body on the floor

The little boy stood up. 'Teacher,' he said 'for a short time this morning we stopped reading and writing and we played in this room. By accident, your table went on the floor and your ink stone broke in half. We felt very bad about that and we wanted to die. So everybody ate some of the poison in your basket. Now we're waiting to die. We're very sorry.'

And he lay down again on the floor.

The teacher didn't speak. He left the room and went into the garden to think. After a minute or two he smiled and said, 'Hmm, those students are learning quickly.'

READING CHECK

Put these sentences in the correct order. Number them 1–8.

a ☐ The teacher comes back. The little boy tells the teacher about the poison.

b ☐ The students open the basket and find the dried fruit in it.

c ☐ The teacher tells the students, 'There is poison in this basket.'

d ☐ The students push over the table and break the ink stone.

e ☐ The teacher leaves the students. He goes to the nearest town.

f ☐ 'The students are learning quickly,' thinks the teacher.

g ☐ The students all lie down on the floor.

h ☐ The students eat the dried fruit.

WORD WORK

Use the letters to make words. Then write the sentences.

a At olosch the students are learning to read and write.

At school the students are learning to read and write.

b The students write with black kin .

. . . .

c The teacher has a creste .

. . . .

d There is something to eat in the kesbta .

. . . .

e Don't eat that apple! There's nopios on it.

. . . .

f The little boy has a good diae .

. . . .

g The teacher was very angry; he got up quickly and shdupe roev his chair.

. . . .

h The students sat on the rfolo and listened to the story.

. . . .

18

GUESS WHAT

The next story is called *A Picture of Tara*. This is Princess Tara from the story.

A PICTURE OF TARA

What happens in the story? Tick the boxes.

Princess Tara . . .	Yes	No
a . . . sees some birds in a fire.	☐	☐
b . . . sees some animals in a fire.	☐	☐
c . . . thinks, 'All men are bad.'	☐	☐
d . . . thinks, 'All women are bad.'	☐	☐
e . . . wants to marry a prince.	☐	☐
f . . . never wants to marry.	☐	☐

A Picture of Tara

PRINCESS Tara loved riding her horse in the **forest** near her father's palace. But one day her horse stopped suddenly. She saw **smoke** in the trees in front of her.

'**Fire**!' she thought. 'I must go up a tree to see it better.'

From the tree she could see everything. The fire moved east very fast. In front of it ran many animals and **birds**. Princess Tara watched one family of birds: the father and mother birds wanted to carry the young birds because they couldn't **fly**. But it wasn't easy, and the fire came nearer and nearer. In the end, the father bird flew away from the fire. But the mother bird stayed with the young birds and died with them.

After that Princess Tara rode sadly back to the palace and she thought about the birds, and about men and women.

'We're no different from those birds,' she said. 'Women think of their children first. But men don't. I'm never going to **marry** one of them.'

So she told everybody in her country: 'I'm never going to marry.'

After some time, a man arrived at the palace and **painted** some pictures for the king. One day he saw the princess in the garden with a book. He painted her secretly because he liked her face. The next morning he left the palace, and he took the picture of Tara with him.

Some months later, a rich king in a far country bought the picture of Tara. He put it in his palace for everyone to see. 'What a beautiful girl!' they all said.

Now this king had a son. He was called Vikram. Vikram

princess the daughter of a king

forest a place with lots of trees

smoke this is white or grey and goes up into the air from a fire

fire this is red and hot, and it burns

bird an animal that can fly through the sky

fly (*past* **flew**) to go through the air

marry to make someone your husband or wife

paint to put different colours on paper to make a picture

looked at the picture of Tara every day, and one day he said to his father, 'I'm going to find that girl and marry her.'

'But my son,' answered the king, 'who is she? Nobody knows.'

'The painter knew her,' said Vikram. 'Where is he?' But nobody could say.

Vikram was very **sad** and the **prime minister's** daughter, Lata, was sorry

for him. '**Prince** Vikram,' she said, 'I can paint well. You know that. So I'm going paint a small picture of the girl's face and then I'm going to look for her.'

'Thank you, Lata,' said Vikram, 'And good luck!'

So the next day Lata painted a new, smaller picture of Tara's face and she left the palace with it. She went to many countries, but nobody knew the girl in the picture. In the end, very far from home, she came to a new country.

When the people there saw the picture, they said, 'Oh yes, that's our Princess Tara. She doesn't want to marry, you know. It's a very good picture of her!'

'Why doesn't Tara want to marry?' Lata asked. But nobody knew.

So Lata went to Tara's palace. 'I'm a painter,' she said to Tara's father, the king. 'Can I do some work for you?'

'What can you paint?' asked the king.

sad not happy

prime minister an important man who helps the king

prince the son of a king

'I like painting people,' answered Lata. 'Shall I paint your children?'

'I have only one daughter,' answered the king sadly. 'Can you paint her?'

'Of course,' said Lata.

At first Tara wasn't interested, but Lata talked to her and in the end the princess said, 'All right! You can paint my picture. But you must talk to me when you are painting.'

So every morning Lata came to paint the picture of Tara and they talked. Soon they were friends.

The day before she finished the picture, Lata asked Tara, 'Why don't you want to marry?'

Tara smiled. 'Everybody asks me that. They don't understand me,' she said. 'But perhaps I can tell my secret to you.' And she told Lata all about the forest fire and the birds. Lata thought quickly.

'I know a prince in a far country,' she said. 'He saw a forest fire, and it changed him, too. Before he saw the fire he was a happy young man, but now he is sad and he doesn't want to marry. I can't tell you about it because it's a secret. But I can paint a picture of it for you.'

'Can I see your picture tomorrow?' said Tara.

Lata painted all night. In her picture she painted a big forest fire and many animals. At the front of the picture stood Prince Vikram and not far from him was a family of **deer**. The father deer was near the fire with the young deer. But the mother deer stood far away from the fire and from her family.

deer (*plural* **deer**) an animal with long legs, that eats grass and leaves, and can run fast

Early next morning, the picture was ready, and Tara came to Lata's room.

'Where's your picture?' asked Tara. 'I couldn't sleep last

night because I wanted to see it.'

'Here it is,' answered Lata. 'Do you like it?'

Tara looked at the picture carefully. 'But the mother deer is not with her family!' she cried. 'Is this picture true?'

'The prince saw this happen,' answered Lata. 'And so now, for him, all women are bad.'

'But not all women are bad,' said Tara. 'The prince is wrong!'

'Is he?' asked Lata. 'Then perhaps you are wrong about men!'

Tara went to her room at once, and nobody saw her again all day.

The next morning she called Lata to her room.

'I would like to meet your prince,' she said. 'Perhaps I can help him.'

Lata smiled. 'You can. I'm sure,' she said. 'Come with me to visit him.'

So what happened when Tara met Vikram? It was true love, of course. And soon after they met, they married and were very happy.

READING CHECK

Match the two parts of the sentences.

a One day Tara sees . . .

b The father bird . . .

c The mother bird . . .

d 'Men are bad,' thinks . . .

e A man paints . . .

f Vikram thinks Tara is . . .

g Lata finds Tara in . . .

h In a picture, Lata tells Tara about . . .

i Tara marries . . .

1 a picture of Tara.

2 Vikram.

3 a forest fire.

4 a new country.

5 dies with the young birds.

6 the father deer.

7 flies away from the fire.

8 Tara.

9 beautiful.

WORD WORK

1 Find words from *A Picture of Tara* to match the pictures.

smoke

b _ _ _

p _ _ _ _ _

f _ _ _ _ _

p _ _ _ _

s _ _

d _ _ _

p _ _ _ _ _ _ _

2 Use the words from Activity 1 to complete the sentences.

a Tara sees a lot of . . .*smoke*. . . from the big fire.

b Tara is very . . . . because the mother . . . . dies in the fire.

c Lata has an idea; she's going to . . . . a picture of Vikram in the . . . .
with a family of . . . .

d At the end of the story . . . . Vikram marries . . . . Tara.

GUESS WHAT

The next story is called *Irka's Well*. Here are the two people in it. Tick the boxes.

Prince Frederick

Irka

a Prince Frederick is . . .

   1 ☐ poor.

   2 ☐ rich.

   3 ☐ sad.

b Irka is . . .

   1 ☐ beautiful.

   2 ☐ rich.

   3 ☐ old.

c The story begins . . .

   1 ☐ near Irka's house.

   2 ☐ at Frederick's palace.

   3 ☐ in the forest.

d In the story Frederick must . . .

   1 ☐ marry Irka.

   2 ☐ paint Irka.

   3 ☐ drink from Irka's shoe.

Irka's Well

Frederick, Prince of Brandenburg, was a rich man. One summer he went to visit a friend in Poland. He rode his horse through forests and by beautiful rivers.

One hot day, he went down the wrong road and arrived in a village far from his friend's house. He was tired, so he stopped near a **cottage** and got off his horse. Next to the cottage was a **well**. Frederick gave his horse some water from the well and then he began to sit down. Just then, someone said, 'Don't sit there!'

The prince looked up and saw a beautiful girl in the cottage garden.
'Did you say something?' he asked her.
'Yes, don't sit there!' she said again.
'Why do you say that?' he asked.
'Because,' said the girl, 'when a man sits by that well, he must marry the girl from this cottage.'

cottage a small house in the country

well a place where you can get water from under the ground

Frederick laughed. 'Is she very **ugly**, this girl?' he asked.
'Oh, no!' said the girl. 'It's me, and my name's Irka.'
Frederick looked at Irka carefully. He liked her beautiful face and her long gold hair.
'I see,' he said. 'I'd like to sit down now. Can I?'
But Irka wasn't happy about it. Frederick looked at Irka. 'What is it now?' he asked angrily. 'Am I ugly?'
'You're rich,' said Irka, 'and I'm poor. You can't marry a poor wife, I'm sure.'
'I have lots of gold,' said Frederick, 'but I like the gold in your hair better than all my gold coins.'
In the end he sat down and Irka smiled.

The wall of the well was warm in the summer sun and Frederick felt very tired. He began to lie down.

'Be careful!' said Irka. 'Don't lie down on that wall!'

ugly not beautiful

Frederick sat up angrily. 'I am a prince,' he answered, 'and when I want to lie down, I lie down.'
'I'm sorry,' said Irka. 'But you don't understand. When a man puts his head on that wall, he must spend half the year in Poland. And you aren't from Poland, I'm sure.'

Frederick thought for a minute. 'Half the year in Poland?' He thought about the rivers and the forests. He looked at the beautiful flowers in Irka's garden. Then he thought about his family and friends in Brandenburg. 'Shall I spend half the year in Poland with my new Polish wife?' he thought.

He put his head down on the wall in the sun and soon he slept. Irka said nothing more. She went into the cottage and made something for her prince to eat.

A month later, Frederick married Irka and everyone came to the **wedding**. They all drank good red **wine** from Frederick's country and laughed when they heard the story of Irka's well.

Suddenly an important Polish prince arrived. He was very late and all the **glasses** were dirty.
'We can't give wine to a prince in a dirty glass!' they said.

The Polish prince understood at once.
'I don't need a glass,' he said. 'I can see something better to drink from.'
He looked at Irka and said, 'Give me one of your shoes.'
Then Frederick put some wine into the shoe.

'I would like everyone to drink from this shoe,' said the Polish prince.
'Let's all drink to Irka and Frederick!'
So everyone drank from Irka's shoe.

And in Poland, for many years after that, people at weddings always drank wine from the **bride's** shoe.

wedding the day when two people marry

wine a red or white drink; when you drink a lot you feel happy and sleepy

glass you drink from this

bride a woman on the day that she marries

READING CHECK

Correct six more mistakes in the story.

                  rich

Prince Frederick is a ~~poor~~ man. One winter he goes to visit a friend in Poland. He goes

down the wrong road and he arrives at a cottage. He is tired and he begins to sit down

by the door. Just then an ugly young woman called Irka comes out of the cottage.

'Don't sit there!' she says. 'When a man sits there, he must kill the girl from the cottage.'

Then Frederick begins to lie down. 'Don't lie down on that wall!' says Irka. 'When a man

puts his head on that wall, he must spend half the year in Italy.'

In the end Frederick marries Irka and at their wedding a Polish prince drinks wine

from Irka's glass.

WORD WORK

Find words from *Irka's Well* to complete the sentences.

b The b _ _ _ _
looks wonderful!

a Would you like
some w i n e ?

No, thank you.
I'd like some
coke, please.

Yes, what a
beautiful dress!

c This is a photo of our w _ _ _ _ _ _ .

You look very happy.

d Be careful! Don't fall down the w _ _ _ !

No, Mummy!

e Oh no! That's your best g _ _ _ _ .

Don't worry. It's OK.

That's my favourite painting. What do you think of it?

f I don't like it. It's really u _ _ _ .

GUESS WHAT

The next story is called *Ali's Wife*. In the story Ali has a sign in his shop about women. What does the sign say? Tick one box.

a
Women are beautiful, but men are cleverer.

b
Women are clever, but men think faster.

c
Women are good, but men are better.

Ali's wife

FATIMA was a beautiful young woman from Syria. One day she saw a big new shop in one of the streets in her home town. On the front of the shop was a **sign**. It said: *Women are **clever**, but men think faster.* 'Who wrote that?' she said angrily. 'Ali, the **shopkeeper**,' people told her. Fatima went into the shop.

'What a nice day!' said Ali.

'Not for me,' answered Fatima and she began to cry.

Ali was **surprised**.

'Why not?' Ali asked. 'What's the matter?'

'Every time a man wants to marry me, my father always tells him, "My daughter is **cross-eyed**, and has big, ugly feet." Is it true?'

She looked at Ali with her big, dark eyes.

'Your eyes are beautiful,' said Ali.

'What about my feet?' she asked sadly.

Ali looked at her feet.

sign writing in a place that tells people something important

clever quick-thinking

shopkeeper somebody who has a shop

surprised feeling that something very new is suddenly happening

cross-eyed with eyes that look in

'They're wonderful feet,' he said. 'Who is your father? I must talk to him.'

'My father is the judge,' answered Fatima, 'the richest man in town.'

'Don't cry any more,' said Ali. 'I'm going to visit him tomorrow. Everything is going to change.'

'But what about when he calls me cross-eyed and talks about my big ugly feet?' said Fatima.

'I'm ready for his stories,' answered Ali. Fatima left the shop and went home.

Ali couldn't sleep all night. Every time he closed his eyes, he saw Fatima's beautiful, dark eyes.

The next day, he got up early and walked quickly to the judge's house. The judge was very surprised when Ali asked to marry his daughter.

'Do you know about my daughter?' he asked. 'She's cross-eyed and has big, ugly feet.'

'That doesn't matter to me,' said Ali.

'But can you pay for her?' asked the judge. 'You must pay 10,000 gold coins to marry her.'

'That's nothing to me,' said Ali. 'I have a big shop. Here's the money.'

So the judge said 'yes' to the wedding.

Later that day, a man came to Ali's door with a big basket. 'This basket is from the judge,' said the man.

'It's her things, I'm sure,' thought Ali. But when he opened the basket, there was an ugly young woman in it. She was cross-eyed and had big, ugly feet.

'Who are you?' asked Ali.

'I'm the judge's daughter,' she answered. 'But I'm going to be your wife.'

Ali sat down suddenly next to the basket. 'So who was the beautiful girl in my shop?' he thought. He gave the ugly young woman something to eat and then went to his room. He didn't understand a thing.

The next morning he opened his shop at the usual time. He sat with his head in his hands. The door opened and Fatima came in.

'Good morning. What a nice day!' she said.

This time Ali cried.

'Not for me,' he said. 'Now I'm going to have an ugly wife. But I wanted to marry you. You're not the judge's daughter!'

'No, my father is the **blacksmith**,' said Fatima.

'Why are you doing this to me?' asked Ali.

'Who thinks faster,' asked Fatima, 'men or women?'

Ali looked at Fatima. 'Ah, now I understand!' he said. 'The sign on the front of my shop . . . !'

With that, Fatima left the shop and went home.

The next day Fatima walked past the shop and looked at the sign. *Men think fast, but women are cleverer*, she read.

She went into the shop. 'That's better!' she said. 'Now, listen to me. I can help you. You're going to have a big wedding for your new wife. Ask the poorest people in town to your house, and ask your bride's father too. When the poor people arrive, tell the judge: "These people are all in my family." He doesn't want any poor people in his family. I'm sure of that.'

Fatima was right. When the judge met the poor people at Ali's house, he was very angry.

'I don't want my daughter to marry someone from this family,' he cried. 'Give her back at once!'

blacksmith a man who works to make metal shoes for horses

34

'But I like her,' said Ali.

'You can have your 10,000 gold coins back' said the judge.

'No thank you,' said Ali.

'What about 20,000 gold coins, then?' asked the judge.

In the end, Ali took the 20,000 gold coins and gave the young woman back to her father.

The next day Ali went to the blacksmith's house. 'I want to marry your daughter,' he said.

'Oh yes?' said the blacksmith.

'But first,' said Ali, 'can I see her? Perhaps you have more than one daughter.'

Fatima's father smiled. 'Fatima,' he called, 'please bring our visitor some coffee.'

When Fatima came in and saw Ali, she laughed.

'Why are you here?' she asked.

'I want to marry the right woman this time,' he said.

Now everybody laughed.

'Let's have some of Fatima's coffee,' said her father.

READING CHECK

Choose the correct pictures.

a One day Fatima sees a . . . in a shop.

b When Fatima goes into the shop she begins to . . . .

c 'Fatima has beautiful . . . ,' thinks Ali.

d At first Fatima says, 'My father is a . . . '

e Ali pays . . . gold coins to marry Fatima.

f When Ali opens the basket he finds a . . . .

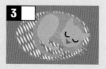

g Fatima's father is really a . . . .

h When the judge sees the poor people at Ali's house he is . . . .

i At the end of the story, Fatima makes a . . . for Ali.

women
are clever
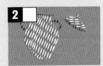

WORD WORK

1 Find four more words from the basket.

2 Use the words from Activity 1 to complete these sentences.

a Fatima's father isn't a judge, he's a
. blacksmith . . .

b Ali has a shop; he's a . . . .

c One day Ali puts a . . . . in
the window of his shop.

d Fatima is a very . . . . woman.
She can think very quickly.

e Ali is very . . . . when a
woman comes out of the basket.

PROJECT A *A traditional wedding*

1 Read about a traditional wedding in Poland and complete the table below.

In Poland men and women marry in their early twenties. The bride wears a long white dress with a veil and the groom wears a smart suit.

Before the ceremony the bride and the groom visit the bride's family. The family give them a loaf of bread, and the couple kiss the bread.

The wedding is usually in a church. After the wedding people throw rice, confetti (small pieces of coloured paper) and coins over the bride and the groom.

Then there is a big wedding dinner for around 100 people. Everyone brings presents of flowers and money for the couple.

When the bride and groom arrive at the wedding dinner they drink some champagne. They then throw their glasses on the floor behind them for good luck. There are a lot of good things to eat and the dinner finishes late in the evening.

Country . . . . Age of the couple . . . .
Bride's clothes . . . .
Grooms' clothes . . . .
Before the wedding . . . .
Place of the wedding . . . .
Wedding dinner . . . .
Presents . . . .
Food and drink . . . .

2 Look at the photographs of two traditional weddings. Which sentences describe the Turkish wedding and which ones describe the Korean wedding? Write *T* or *K* in the box.

a The bride is wearing a white dress.

b The groom is wearing a black hat.

c The bride is signing her name in the wedding book.

d The groom is pouring some wine for the bride to drink.

e There are lots of good things to eat on the table.

3 Describe a wedding in your country. Complete the table below.

Country . . . . Age of the couple . . . .

Bride's clothes . . . .

Grooms' clothes . . . .

Before the wedding . . . .

Place of the wedding . . . .

Wedding dinner . . . .

Presents . . . .

Food and drink . . . .

4 Make a poster about weddings in your country.

PROJECT B *Telling a story*

1 Aesop's fables are famous stories about animals. Read this story about the fox and the crow. Match the sentences with the pictures.

a ☐ One day a big black crow sat a tree. She had some nice yellow cheese in her beak.

b ☐ A fox saw the cheese in the crow's beak, so he came and sat under the tree. 'I'm very hungry,' he thought. 'How can I get that cheese?' Then the fox said to the crow, 'You're a beautiful bird! Can you sing beautifully, too?'

c ☐ The crow listened carefully to the fox. 'Yes, I can sing beautifully,' she thought, and she began to sing noisily.

d ☐ The cheese fell to the floor and the fox ate it at once. 'Thank you. You sing beautifully,' he said to the crow. (It wasn't true.) 'But you aren't very clever!' laughed the fox.

2 Complete the story of Princess Tara with the words below.

> *after some time ◆ at once ◆ but ◆ so ◆ but*
> *in the end ◆ but ◆ that night ◆ one day*

(a) . . . . Princess Tara saw a family of birds in a forest fire near her palace. The father bird flew away from the young birds **(b)** . . . . the mother stayed with them and died. Princess Tara thought about the father bird and she said, 'I'm never going to marry.'

(c) . . . . a man arrived at the palace and he secretly painted a picture of Tara. Some months later Prince Vikram saw the picture. He wanted to marry the beautiful woman **(d)** . . . . nobody knew her name.

The prime minister's daughter, Lata, was sorry for Vikram **(e)** . . . . she went to many different countries and found Tara. Lata painted Tara's picture and soon they were friends.

Lata asked Tara 'Why don't you want to marry?' and Tara told her all about the forest fire. **(f)** . . . . Lata quickly painted a picture of Prince Vikram and some deer in a fire. The mother deer was not with her family. 'Vikram now thinks all women are bad,' said Lata. '**(g)** . . . . not all women are bad. The prince is wrong!' said Tara. 'Well, perhaps you are wrong about men!' said Lata.

Tara went to her room. The next morning she came out. 'Can I meet Prince Vikram?' she asked.

(h) . . . . Tara and Vikram met, and of course they fell in love **(i)** . . . .

3 Look at the pictures on page 42. Tell the story of the fox and the stork. Use these words and a dictionary to help you.

> *couldn't eat ◆ fed up ◆ flat bowl of soup ◆ fox ◆ invite (someone) to dinner*
> *laugh at (someone) ◆ long beak ◆ stork ◆ tall jug ◆ wave goodbye*

a

b

c

d

e

f

GRAMMAR

GRAMMAR CHECK

When + Past Simple

We use when to link two Past Simple sentences to show two actions that happen close in time in the past. Often the later action is the result of the when action.

King Marco got a letter from King Luca. His oldest daughter wanted to fight.

When King Marco got a letter from King Luca, his oldest daughter wanted to fight.

With when at the start of the sentence, we put a comma after the first clause.

1 **Match sentences a–h with 1–8 and write complete sentences using *when*.**

a ☐7 The oldest daughter saw some trees.

When the oldest daughter saw some trees, she wanted to cook dinner.

b ☐ The second daughter saw a river.

....

c ☐ Fanta Ghirò went into the sword room.

....

d ☐ Fanta Ghirò picked a flower.

....

e ☐ Fanta Ghirò had dinner.

....

f ☐ Fanta Ghirò rode home.

....

g ☐ Fanta Ghirò arrived home.

....

h ☐ King Luca saw that Fanta Ghirò was a woman.

....

1 She put on women's clothes.

2 He asked her to marry him.

3 King Luca went after her.

4 She broke her bread with her hands.

5 She wanted to wash shirts.

6 She put it behind her ear.

7 She wanted to cook dinner.

8 She looked at the swords for hours.

GRAMMAR CHECK

Modal auxiliary verbs: can and can't

We use can + infinitive without *to* to describe things that we are able to do or that are possible.

Ahmet can hear Nasreddin over the garden wall.

We use can't + infinitive without *to* to describe things that we are not able to do or that are not possible.

Nasreddin's wife can't stop talking about money.

2 Put the words in the correct order to make affirmative or negative sentences with *can*.

a can / Nasreddin's wife / with one thousand gold coins / be happy

.....Nasreddin's wife can be happy with one thousand.....
.....gold coins...

b can't / Ahmet / Nasreddin / understand

....

c can / laughing and singing / hear / in Nasreddin's house / Ahmet

....

d because there aren't / have / Nasreddin / can't / one thousand coins exactly / the gold

....

e give / can't / back to Ahmet / the gold / Nasreddin

....

f to court / Nasreddin / can't / in dirty clothes / go

....

g wear / Nasreddin / Ahmet's coat / can

....

h can't / to court / walk / Nasreddin

....

i ride / Nasreddin / Ahmet's horse / can

....

GRAMMAR CHECK

Present Continuous

We use the Present Continuous to talk about things happening now.

We make the Present Continuous with the verb be + the –ing form of the verb.

➕ *The students are studying at a school in Korea.*

➖ *The teacher isn't smiling.* *We aren't learning Chinese.*

❓ *What is the teacher eating?* *What are the students doing?*

We make the –ing form of the verb by adding –ing to the infinitive without *to*. When verbs end in –e, we remove the e and add –ing.

smile – smiling *write – writing*

When short verbs end in consonant + vowel + consonant, we double the final consonant and add –ing.

sit – sitting *swim – swimming*

3 **Look at the picture and complete the text with the verbs in brackets. Use the Present Continuous affirmative, negative, or question form.**

The students a) .....*are sitting*.... (sit) on the floor. They b) .... (learn) to read and write Chinese. The teacher c) .... (watch) his students at work. The students d) .... (not / talk) because they are afraid of their teacher. The teacher e) .... (eat) some dried fruit from a basket. One of the students f) .... (look) at the fruit. He g) .... (ask) the teacher a question: 'What h) .... (you / eat), Teacher?'

GRAMMAR CHECK

Present Simple: third person –s

We add –s to the infinitive without *to* to make the third person (*he/she/it*) form of the Present Simple.

A man arrives at the palace and paints some pictures.

We use **doesn't** + infinitive without *to* to make the third person negative form.

She doesn't want to marry.

When verbs end in –o, –ch, –ss, or –sh, we add –es to make the third person form.

does, watches, kisses, pushes

When verbs end in consonant + –y, we change the y to i and add –es.

cry – cries

We can use the Present Simple tense to re-tell a story.

4 **Complete the sentences re-telling the story of *A Picture of Tara*. Use the verbs in the box in the Present Simple.**

ask	buy	finish	go	look	marry	meet
paint	not stay	talk	not tell	think	not want	

a A rich king in a far away country .buys. the picture of Tara.

b His son Vikram .... at the picture every day.

c Lata .... a smaller picture of Tara and then she .... to many countries.

d Finally Lata comes to a new country and she .... people who know Princess Tara.

e Lata speaks to Tara's father and he .... her to paint Tara's picture.

f Lata paints and .... to Tara every day, so soon they are friends.

g Before Lata .... the picture, Tara tells her the story of the forest fire and why she .... to marry.

h Lata .... Tara Vikram's story; she paints it.

i Tara looks at the picture carefully. In the picture the mother deer .... with the young deer.

j Vikram .... that women are bad so he doesn't want to marry.

k In the end Tara meets Vikram and soon after she .... him.

GRAMMAR CHECK

Modal auxiliary verbs: can't, must, and would like

We use can't + infinitive without *to* to describe actions that we are not able to do or that are not possible.

Prince Frederick can't find his friend's house because he went down the wrong road.

We use must + infinitive without *to* to describe actions that we have to do or that are an obligation.

When a man sits by the well he must marry the girl from the cottage.

We use would like + to + infinitive to describe actions that we want to do.

Prince Frederick would like to sit down because he's tired.

5 Correct the mistakes in the sentences.

a Prince Frederick would like ^to^ visit his friends in Poland.

b Irka says, 'You can't to sit there.'

c Frederick must marrying Irka because he sits by the well.

d Frederick is tired so he like to lie down.

e Frederick lies down on the wall so he musts spend half the year in Poland.

f The Polish prince can't any wine because the glasses are dirty.

6 Complete the sentences using *can't, must,* or *would like.*

a Prince Frederick _must_ marry Irka because he sits down by the well.

b Irka .... marry Prince Frederick because she is very poor.

c Prince Frederick thinks that Irka is beautiful so he .... to marry her.

d Prince Frederick .... spend half the year in Poland when he puts his head on the wall.

e Prince Frederick .... to live in Poland because Irka lives there.

f The Polish prince .... drink from a wine glass because all the glasses are dirty.

g The Polish prince doesn't need a glass because he .... to drink from Irka's shoe.

GRAMMAR CHECK

Have got: affirmative and negative

We use have got to express possession.

We use have/has + got to make the affirmative form.

The judge has got an ugly daughter.

We use haven't/hasn't + got to make the negative form.

The judge hasn't got a beautiful daughter.

We use have got to express possession in the Present Simple only.

7 **Complete the sentences using *have got* affirmative or negative.**

a Ali / a big shop

.....Ali has got a big shop.....

b Ali / a lot of carpets

....

c Fatima / beautiful eyes

....

d Fatima / big feet

....

e The judge's daughter / beautiful eyes

....

f The judge / a lot of money

....

g The judge / poor people in his family

....

h The blacksmith / two daughters

....

i The blacksmith / a clever daughter

....